Curriculum Visions Explorers

Exploring
climate
chaos

A view of Hurricane
Katrina approaching the
USA in 2005. More large
hurricanes are forecast
in the years ahead.

Dr Brian Knapp

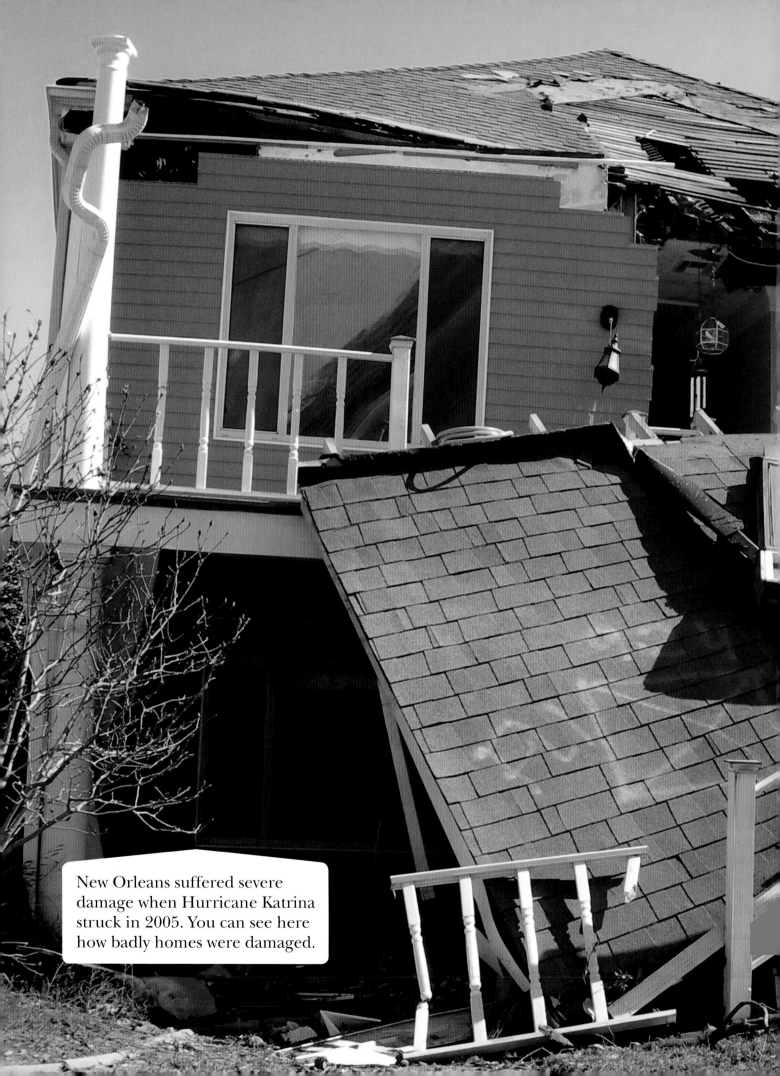

New Orleans suffered severe damage when Hurricane Katrina struck in 2005. You can see here how badly homes were damaged.

Contents

Look up the **bold** words in the glossary
on page 32 of this book.

Is our climate really in chaos?

You may have heard much about the way our **climate** is changing. People don't mean changes from day to day – that is called the weather. What they mean is what we think of as a normal year, will not be the same in the future.

The average kinds of summer and winter we get will change. Some people will face **drought** and be on the verge of starvation.

Others will face far more floods and storms than in the past. This book is about explaining how we have brought about this change, what we can do, and what will happen if we don't.

If the Earth's clouds move in different ways, then some places might get drought and other places might get floods.

Did you know... ?

- The world's temperature is rising. Two thirds of the rise in the last century has been in the last 30 years.
- The 1990s were the warmest 10-year period since records began in England in the 1660s, and the 2000s are almost sure to be warmer still.
- Sea level is rising by a metre a century.
- Much of the change in climate over the next 30 to 40 years is already set by what we have done in the past. We will just have to put up with it.
- The climate after this will be set by what we do today. So, our future is partly in our hands.

Q **Why are clouds important?**

The Earth's edge

If you look at the Earth from space, you see a thin, blue hazy band between the Earth's surface and space. This is called the Earth's **atmosphere**. It contains all of the air we use to breathe, and it is what keeps us safe from the direct rays of the Sun. It also helps to hold the heat, saving us from being a frozen planet.

From the ground the atmosphere seems huge. It is everything we can see in the sky. But from space you can see it is very thin. This is why we can change it, and when we change it, we help to change our climate – often for the worse.

This is a view showing Europe.

This is what the atmosphere looks like at sunset if you fly high in the sky. It is the blue haze above the orange clouds. Above that is the blackness of space.

Did you know… ?

- The part of the atmosphere which has the clouds in is just 18 km thick (just twice the height of Mt Everest).
- The layer above the cloud zone is called the **stratosphere**. It is like an invisible lid, holding our weather and gases close to the surface. It reaches up to 50 km above the Earth.
- The air is made of a mixture of invisible gases. The air is just over three quarters nitrogen and a fifth oxygen. The tiny amount left is mainly water vapour, carbon dioxide and methane. These gases hold the key to climate change.

Q What is the atmosphere?

How are we causing change?

The Earth's climate varies naturally from year to year and century to century, and we have to take this into account. But even so, we have seen a steady rise in temperature on top of this natural change. That is due to us and this is why.

The air is made up of many gases that are invisible, so we can't see them. The oxygen we use to breathe is one of these gases. Most of these gases have no effect on the Earth's heat but some do. They are called carbon dioxide, methane and water vapour (moisture).

Carbon dioxide is a mixture of **carbon** and oxygen. This is the gas that is made in our lungs and we breathe it out. Methane also contains carbon.

These gases soak up heat, making all the air warmer. The more of these gases there are in the air, the warmer it will get.

The gases that contain carbon are so important in this that they are called greenhouse gases.

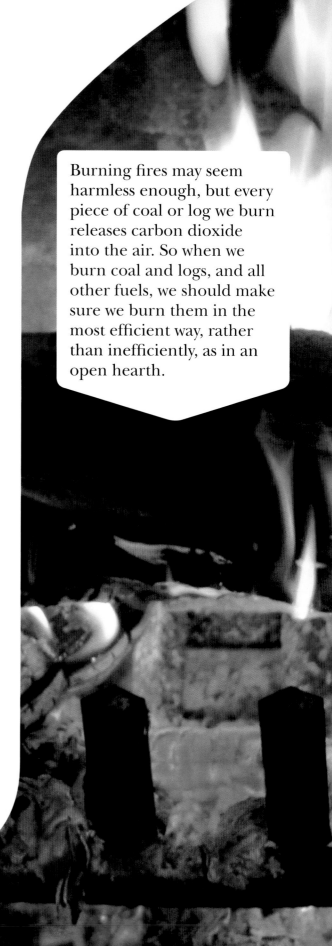

Burning fires may seem harmless enough, but every piece of coal or log we burn releases carbon dioxide into the air. So when we burn coal and logs, and all other fuels, we should make sure we burn them in the most efficient way, rather than inefficiently, as in an open hearth.

Shipping and aircraft are the fastest-growing carbon producers.

Did you know… ?

- An average UK family releases about 25 tons of carbon into the air each year (home and car combined). This is equivalent to about 50 large sacks of coal.
- An average American family releases about 45 tons of carbon into the air each year (home and car combined). This is equivalent to about 90 large sacks of coal.
- Much of the methane released into the air comes from grazing animals like cows. They release it as they digest the grass. Much also comes from rubbish dumps and is produced as rubbish decays.

Q **Which are the two fastest growing producers of carbon?**

Sun

The way that heat moves in the air.

Some heat escapes into space

The Sun's rays warm the Earth

Cloud

Did you know... ?

- The greenhouse effect is what makes the Earth warm enough for life to grow here. If it weren't for the gases trapping the warmth from the Sun, the Earth would be too cold for life.
- Sunlight passes through the air without heating it.
- The sunlight warms the ground. The heat from the ground is then shared with the air and is soaked up by gases in the air like carbon dioxide.

Earth

What 'greenhouse Earth' means

In a greenhouse in a garden, sunshine gets through the glass and warms up the air inside. This heat soaked up by the air cannot escape because of the glass, so the inside of a greenhouse gets warmer and warmer. In the Earth, carbon dioxide and methane gases soak up heat, which is why they are called greenhouse gases.

To make sure that the Earth's temperature remains suitable for life, the balance of these gases in the air must not be upset. But we have tipped the balance. When we burn trees, coal, oil or gas, we get energy, but we also put carbon dioxide into the air.

Carbon dioxide is soaked up by plants and trees. The oceans also soak up these gases, but we are now releasing more carbon dioxide by burning fuels than the trees and the oceans can soak up.

Q What is the most important greenhouse gas?

Some heat that would otherwise leave the Earth and go into space is trapped by greenhouse gases and makes the air warmer.

Measuring carbon

How do we measure what we are doing? Carbon dioxide is a gas, and coal is a solid, so how do we compare solids and gases? Carbon is found in both of them so we look to see how much carbon is in the air and how much is in coal, oil, natural gas and so on. These measures can be compared.

We then find that the world's people send an incredible 6.5 billion tons of carbon into the air each year.

4.5 billion tons of the total is from burning coal, oil and natural gas for energy. We are also cutting down and burning forests that would have soaked up some of this carbon. This is the same as if we burned another 2 billion tons of carbon each year.

Trains

This diagram shows the main sources of greenhouse gases in the air.

Burning forest

Aircraft

Did you know... ?

• Heat comes into the Earth and it goes out again. But this all takes a long time to change because the amounts stored by the Earth are immense. So we should expect what we have done in the past to take 30 to 40 years to work its way through. That means that what we do today will affect what the climate is like more than 40 years from now.

Q What forms of energy do you use everyday?

Power stations

Factories

Homes

Car and truck exhaust

Ships

Animals

13

What winter will be like

With more storms forecast in winter, ships driven aground might well be a more common sight.

In the UK winters will be warmer and up to three times wetter.

There will be many more very wet days; the sort of days that make rivers burst their banks and cause flooding.

We will see fewer very cold winters, much less frost, and snowfall will be less. Many of us will not see any snow during winter.

Did you know… ?

- If temperatures do not fall below 6°C many plants carry on growing and produce their flowers too early. They then get stressed and are less able to grow strongly.
- Lack of snow may be very bad news for the tourist industry.
- More storms will mean that insurance companies will charge more.

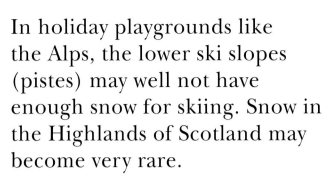

In holiday playgrounds like the Alps, the lower ski slopes (pistes) may well not have enough snow for skiing. Snow in the Highlands of Scotland may become very rare.

Autumn and winter will get windier, with more damaging storms.

Winters will get shorter and may not go below the temperature at which plants stop growing (6°C). Winters in the future may be more like the Mediterranean countries get today.

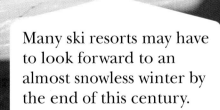

Many ski resorts may have to look forward to an almost snowless winter by the end of this century.

How might tourists be affected by climate change?

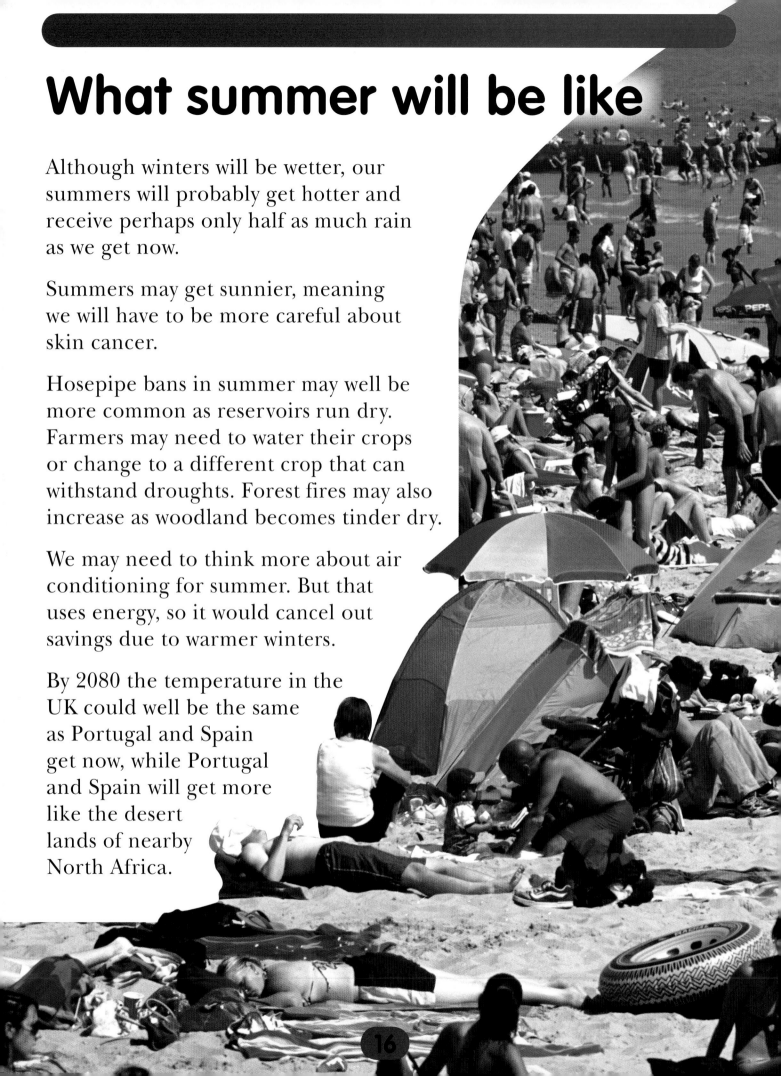

What summer will be like

Although winters will be wetter, our summers will probably get hotter and receive perhaps only half as much rain as we get now.

Summers may get sunnier, meaning we will have to be more careful about skin cancer.

Hosepipe bans in summer may well be more common as reservoirs run dry. Farmers may need to water their crops or change to a different crop that can withstand droughts. Forest fires may also increase as woodland becomes tinder dry.

We may need to think more about air conditioning for summer. But that uses energy, so it would cancel out savings due to warmer winters.

By 2080 the temperature in the UK could well be the same as Portugal and Spain get now, while Portugal and Spain will get more like the desert lands of nearby North Africa.

Sunbathing at Bournemouth during the 2003 heat wave. Temperatures in the low 30s will probably no longer be thought of as a heat wave in the future.

Did you know... ?

- We will continue to break all records for high temperatures.
- The warming will not be even: nights will get warmer faster and we will have many hot, sticky summer nights.
- Heat waves will be more and more common.
- Summer will come sooner and last longer into what we now think of as winter.
- Holidaying abroad may slow down as Mediterranean summers become unbearably hot.

Q Why might we stop going to the Mediterranean for our holidays?

The hurricane called Katrina which flooded much of the American city of New Orleans in 2005 and blew down many houses happened in a year when more hurricanes were recorded than ever before.

Q **What else can we expect besides flooding?**

More extreme weather

Sometimes the weather becomes very violent and frightening indeed. Giant tidal waves, hurricanes, tornadoes and floods are all due to the weather.

The reason we will have more storms, more flooding and more hurricanes is that the more heat we put in the air, the more energy there is for the wind to get stronger and for the air to hold more moisture, then get rid of it as violent storms. As the seas get hotter they will get hot enough to start hurricanes more often, too.

Change will not just be in winter winds and storms. It will be in summer heat waves and droughts. Heat waves will become fifteen times more common in the Scottish Highlands than they are today.

More extreme weather doesn't just mean trees blown down. It affects where we shall live. When you build a house you expect it to last for centuries. But in the future we may not be able to build where we have built in the past.

Did you know... ?

- There is a current of hot water in the tropics that can affect the weather all around the world. It is called El Niño.
- El Niño moves backwards and forwards across the Pacific Ocean every four or five years and can bring unusual floods and droughts. Now it seems to be happening more often.
- The 1997 El Niño had more energy than a million atomic bombs. By the time it had run its course after eight months it had changed weather patterns around the world, killed 2,100 people, and caused at least $20 billion in property damage.

What will suffer most?

Many wild plants will not be able to stand these changes and they will die, to be replaced by plants more suited to this new weather.

As warmth spreads towards the poles, there will be nowhere for the animals who live in the cold to go. Polar bears, for example, could become extinct.

The world's seas will rise as the warmer conditions make the ice in the Arctic, Antarctica and Greenland melt. The sea may rise by over half a metre in the next 50 years, making coastal cities more liable to flooding. Bigger storms will add to this problem.

Did you know... ?

- Plants and animals that need cold weather will suffer most and many could die out.
- Polar bears depend on the Arctic sea ice to get out to places where they catch their prey. If the ice melts they will no longer be able to feed, and might starve.

The Arctic sea ice might melt away.

The polar ice cap

Q Why might polar bears become extinct?

Will the change just affect us?

No. It will affect everyone on Earth.

In fact, in our country we will probably get off lightly. It will get hotter and drier in summer, but we should be able to cope.

It is likely that the deserts will grow wider and this means that the billion people living *near* to deserts may, in the future, find themselves *in* the desert as the desert spreads.

Gradually crops will fail and there will not be enough food.

First and foremost, these people will not have enough water. Then they will not have enough food. They will look to us to help them; they will look to move from the lands where they are distressed to lands where the problem is not as bad.

In this way we will all become involved.

Drought means that many plants will die back and there will not be enough food for people or wildlife. As a result, many deaths will occur.

How can we cope if a billion people have too little food?

Did you know... ?

- The Sahara Desert is expanding southwards at around 50 kilometres a year. So, if the desert were at Birmingham, it would reach London in three years time. How would we cope? Now you can see the scale of the problem.

What can we do?

We have already put so much carbon dioxide into the air that things will not get better even if we stay as we are. We have to put less into the air in future. Much less. In fact it means cutting down by two thirds. It is a huge change, and at the moment we are doing virtually nothing at all, so the longer this goes on, the more we will have to change later.

Think of simply the journey to school. If my family drives a big car on the school run I put about 250 grammes of carbon into the air every kilometre. If I drive a small car on the school run it is about 150.

The petrol or diesel my car uses contains the carbon that the engine needs to make energy, so we can't strain the carbon out.

Getting ready for a shared school run.

If I drive 20,000 km a year (an average figure) then the amount of carbon I send out into the air is 20,000 x 250g for a big car and 20,000 x 150g for a small car. That is 5000kg, or 5 tons (5 times the weight of the car). For a small car it is 3 tons, still probably 5 times the weight of the car!

Did you know... ?

- Idling a car for more than half a minute burns more fuel than it takes to restart the engine.
- Always replacing your car with one that does more miles to the gallon will save carbon, and encourage more economical cars to be made.

So if I drove less by sharing journeys with friends, I would produce less carbon. It is that simple.

Q How much carbon a year do you burn on your school run?

It takes time to make giant power stations more efficient because new ways have to be found, so we should NOT look to them to make quick changes.

Can we balance our use of carbon?

We are putting more carbon into the air than we are taking out. So is there a way to take as much out as we put in?

Some people have suggested that we can balance our carbon. Every company gets a **quota** of how much carbon they can produce. Those companies who send out more carbon can buy 'carbon credits' from those who use less. But it does nothing to encourage anyone to use less.

In any case, it is not just the fault of businesses. Energy companies supply us with oil, natural gas and electricity. So if we demand energy, we are causing more carbon to go into the air. So it is not someone else's problem, it is also ours at home.

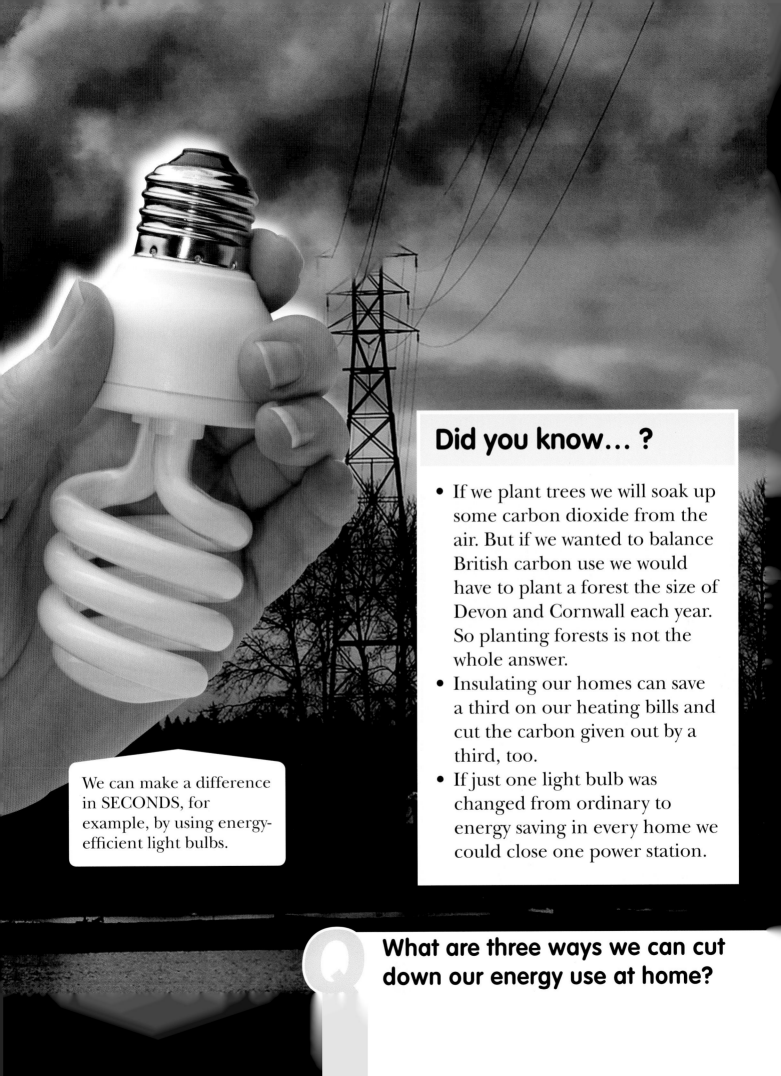

Did you know… ?

- If we plant trees we will soak up some carbon dioxide from the air. But if we wanted to balance British carbon use we would have to plant a forest the size of Devon and Cornwall each year. So planting forests is not the whole answer.
- Insulating our homes can save a third on our heating bills and cut the carbon given out by a third, too.
- If just one light bulb was changed from ordinary to energy saving in every home we could close one power station.

We can make a difference in SECONDS, for example, by using energy-efficient light bulbs.

What are three ways we can cut down our energy use at home?

Help the developing world

We are very fortunate. We live comfortably. We have everything we need.

But other people are not so lucky. However, they now have a chance to get some of the things we take for granted. People in India and China, for example, can now afford electricity when they could not in the past. More of them can afford cars or motorbikes.

Should we tell them they can't have what we have?

Electricity, cars and motorbikes use energy and so give out greenhouse gases.

Soon India and China will produce more carbon than any country (even more than the USA, which is the biggest producer of greenhouse gases today).

As people become wealthier they want cars. As a result, they put more carbon dioxide into the air.

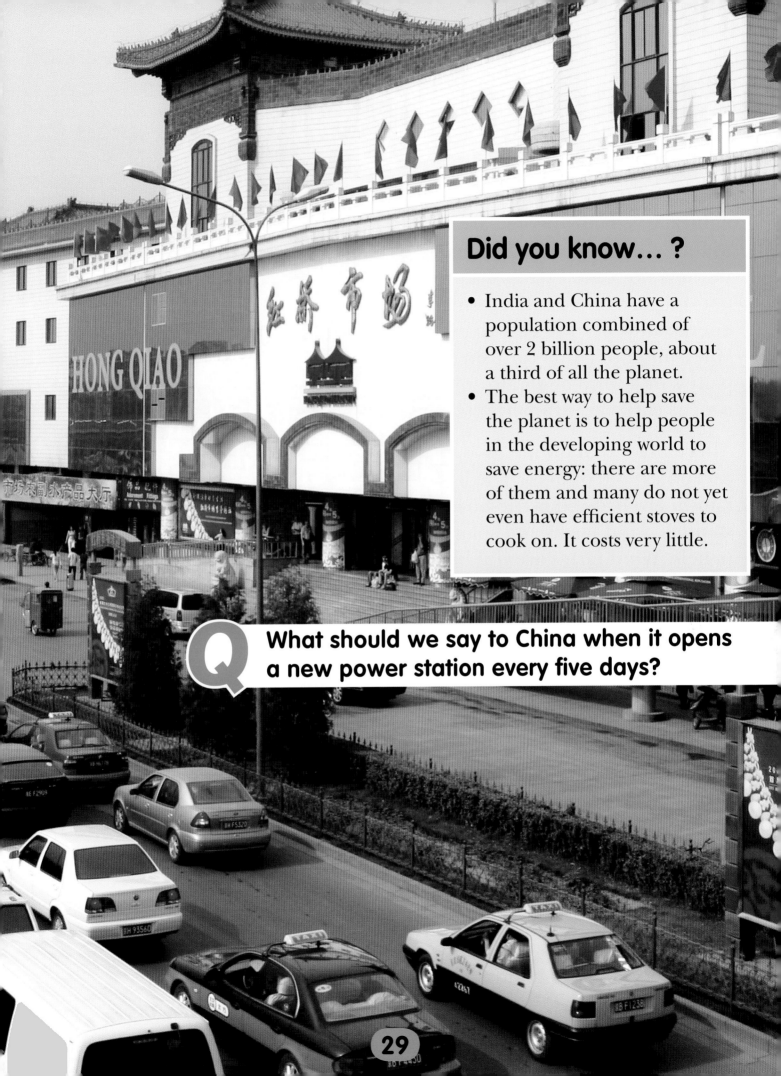

Did you know... ?

- India and China have a population combined of over 2 billion people, about a third of all the planet.
- The best way to help save the planet is to help people in the developing world to save energy: there are more of them and many do not yet even have efficient stoves to cook on. It costs very little.

Q What should we say to China when it opens a new power station every five days?

Are there alternatives?

Because so much of the problem is caused by burning coal, oil and natural gas, many people are trying to find alternative kinds of energy. But it is not easy. Coal, oil and natural gas are very rich forms of energy and they are easy to use. You could not run a car using solar panels or a wind generator on its roof as easily as with petrol.

Alternatives that do not give out carbon can be of help. The best known are hydro-electric power stations, wind farms and solar panels. Wind farms are not likely to be useful in the long run for most countries. Solar panels will get more efficient as they are developed. Using hydrogen as a fuel may be more promising. Nuclear power is also an option because it does not release any carbon dioxide. We should also remember that if we could make everything two thirds more efficient, we would go a long way to solving our problem.

We can use wind turbines.

We can make more use of the Sun to make electricity.

Did you know... ?

- If we cut back by two thirds today air temperatures will still rise for several tens of years and sea levels would keep rising for several centuries. It all takes time.
- We could never use renewable energy alone because it only works, for example, when the Sun shines or when the wind blows, yet we need energy all the time. This is why we will still need ordinary power stations and why some people think nuclear power is a good option.

We can harness more rivers to make hydro-electric power.

Q **Which produces a continuous amount of electricity: wind, nuclear or solar?**

Glossary

atmosphere A scientist's word for the air above the Earth's surface. It is made up of many invisible gases. The oxygen we breathe is one of these gases, carbon dioxide that causes climate change is another.

carbon Carbon is one of the building blocks of all life. It is called an element. Carbon combines with many other building blocks to make new substances. For example carbon is found in coal and soot. But carbon is not found in black things. It combines to make substances including all of our bodies (bones as well as flesh), all plant tissues, all fuels, carbon dioxide and methane gases.

climate The average weather we might expect. Even though the climate is changing, one year will still be different from another. Climate change means that, on average, the years will be warmer, although any one year might still be cool.

drought An unusually long period without rain. Many parts of the world have months without rain. This is called a dry season and is normal. But if a time that is supposed to be rainy proves to be dry, then that is unusual and is called a drought. In the UK a drought is often thought of as 30 days without rain. That is because we expect rain every month and so a month without rain is unusual.

quota A fixed amount, a kind of ration.

stratosphere The part of the atmosphere above where the clouds and weather occur. It acts like an invisible lid, holding greenhouse gases close to the Earth.

Index

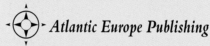

Curriculum Visions

Curriculum Visions is a registered trademark of Atlantic Europe Publishing Company Ltd.

Atlantic Europe Publishing

Curriculum Visions Explorers
This series provides straightforward introductions to key worlds and ideas.

You might also be interested in
Our larger book, 'Weather around the world'. There is a Teacher's Guide to match 'Weather around the world'. Additional notes in PDF format are also available from the publisher to support 'Exploring climate chaos'. All of these products are suitable for KS2.

Dedicated Web Site
Watch movies, see many more pictures and read much more in detail about weather-related topics at:

www.curriculumvisions.com
(Professional Zone: subscription required)

First published in 2007 by Atlantic Europe Publishing Company Ltd
Copyright © 2007 Earthscape

All rights reserved. No part of this publication may be reproduced, stored in a retrieval system, or transmitted in any form or by any means, electronic, mechanical, photocopying, recording or otherwise, without prior permission of the publisher.

Author
Brian Knapp, BSc, PhD

Educational Consultant
JM Smith (former Deputy Head of Wellfield School, Burnley, Lancashire)

Senior Designer
Adele Humphries, BA

Editor
Gillian Gatehouse

Photographs
The Earthscape Picture Library, except (t=top, b=bottom, l=left, r=right): NASA p6–7, 21br, 29; ShutterStock p4–5, 9tl, 14–15, 20–21, 22–23, 26–27, 28–29; US Navy p1, 2–3, 18–19.

Acknowledgements
The publishers would like to thank Heidi, Madeleine and Emilia Allen, and Kezia and Jared Humphries

Illustrations
David Woodroffe

Designed and produced by
Earthscape

Printed in China by
WKT Company Ltd

Exploring climate chaos
– Curriculum Visions
A CIP record for this book is available from the British Library

Paperback ISBN 978 1 86214 212 1
Hardback ISBN 978 1 86214 213 8

This product is manufactured from sustainable managed forests. For every tree cut down at least one more is planted.